Thinking Like a Citizen

What Color Am I?

Kathy Swan • S.G. Grant • Emma Thacker
Illustrations by **Peter Francis**

SAVVAS
LEARNING COMPANY

ISBN-13: 978-0-328-78692-3
ISBN-10:   0-328-78692-6
14 20

Ms. Stanton's class was preparing for the school art gallery. They decided to draw pictures of themselves.

6

8

Well, I'm a person and people come in different colors, sooooo . . . I think we should start with the People lenses.

Good thinking. People it is.

9

Genie-what?

I know that word. My family is from Ecuador and my dad likes to look on the computer to see where my great-great-great-great-grandparents came from.

I get it, Zeb. I think we need the Time lenses.

Genealogy is learning about people and where they come from. My family came from Germany a long **time** ago.

Has my family always been the same color?

My mom says we came from Africa a long, long **time** ago, but that's all we know.

12

We have a family tree kind of like this at my house. It shows the names of people in my family from *way* back in **time**.

I wonder where my family comes from and how long we've lived here?

I know what that means— Space lenses.

My mom doesn't look like my dad. She says people treat her differently because of her skin color, and it's harder for her to get a job.

That's not fair!

Aren't there **rules** and laws against that?

16

17

Yeah, Grayson has all the superhero action figures and I only have one.

It's not like you *need* all the action figures, Zeb! You just *want* them.

How do *you* choose the crayons to color yourself?

22

Questions to Talk or Write About

Stuff How do you decide if you need something or just want it?

Rules Do we need rules about how to treat each other? Why or why not?

People Why do you think people don't all look the same?

Time Has your family lived here a long time?

Space Where else has your family lived?